The Heronry

poems

Mark Jarman

SARABANDE BOOKS   LOUISVILLE, KY

Library of Congress Cataloging-in-Publication Data

Names: Jarman, Mark, 1952- author.
Title: The heronry : poems / Mark Jarman.
Description: First edition. | Louisville, KY : Sarabande Books, [2017]
Identifiers: LCCN 2016014118 (print) | LCCN 2016020095 (ebook) | ISBN
9781941411353 (softcover : acid-free paper) | ISBN 9781941411360
Subjects: | BISAC: NATURE / Ecology. | RELIGION / Spirituality. | BODY, MIND
& SPIRIT / Meditation.
Classification: LCC PS3560.A537 A6 2017 (print) | LCC PS3560.A537 (ebook) |
DDC 811/.54—dc23
LC record available at https://lccn.loc.gov/2016014118

Interior and exterior design by Kristen Radtke.

Manufactured in Canada.
This book is printed on acid-free paper.

Sarabande Books is a nonprofit literary organization.

This project is supported in part by an award from the National Endowment for the Arts. The Kentucky Arts
Council, the state arts agency, supports Sarabande Books with state tax dollars and federal funding from the
National Endowment for the Arts.

Contents

The Heronry

Believers, Unbelievers

Will the circle be unbroken?
Bo Dee Jarman (1930–2012)

The Heronry

Ruby Throated Moses

When my eye caught the green surprise
of a hummingbird inside the dim garage,
        like a brooch pinned against the sheetrock wall,
I canted open the creaking garage door
        and tossed him back to blinding summer life.
He spiraled into brilliance, out of sight.

When Michelangelo struck Moses' knee
and shouted at him, "Speak!," the chisel made
        a dent. But Moses kept his glaring silence.
And yet, through the statue's marble hair, a wildness
        stuck out two ridged horns and spoke.
"Let this be light," it said. "Let this be light."

Cul-de-Sac Idyll

The flycatcher feeds its young a lightning bug, frantically blinking.
The trees forget the hurricane as they stand still for days.
The defibrillator sleeps in a lump under our neighbor's shirt pocket.

The flycatcher snagging its prey squirms like a trout in midair.
The dogwoods this spring blew all their savings on taffeta.
The cardiac muscle fibers shudder like untimed pistons.

The flycatcher's beak is a leggy mouthful of bent pins.
The poplars go first, brown-bagging their leaves, one by one.
One false move and the defibrillator kicks like a hoof.

There are words that stop and start sunlight, moonlight, and starlight,
verbs like the motion of thought, nouns like dreams and daydreams,
and the end of the world, and the end of the end, right here.

Bat

I remember the Sierra pond
where at evening bats went dipping,
    pilgrims with sharp chins dipping
to holy water, preying
    on mosquitoes as if praying.
I watched them envying their purpose,
    wanting at twenty some purpose.
Snap the hatchling as it rises,
    skim the darkness as it rises.
I wanted that perfected arc,
    hunting life along an arc,
both creature and creator.

What is it now about the creature
appearing at a sudden angle,
    wavering through dusk, angel
of hunger at the night's rim,
    like a card flicked at a hat brim?
Now I read it like an icon
    blinking on a screen and ken
something there that's meaningful,
    a little void that's never full.

Catch and Release

By the scientist's front door
an azalea, memento
of a term in college catching
field mice under redwoods among
azaleas, to study traits
of families, their range among
azaleas. Now she has one
flowering yearly by her front door.
Pressure of the lab, of funding
overheads and uncommitted
assistants, yet the azalea
greets her every day, a memory
tangled in it like cobweb mist
of doing a simple task
repeatedly, under the redwoods
with the Havahart traps, then in
the clean lit lab. Simplicity,
youth, one or two obligations,
their emblem the azalea.
And the release, gray and silver
quickness in the undergrowth,
to hunting, breeding, hunger—
the speed of life.

Eocene Beech Leaf

This ghost filled in with stone for flesh,
with spine and delicate ribs legible
and a fragment of the fragile blade chipped off,
this leaf imprinted on a page of shale,
all the more tender for its injury,
for forty million years has held its place.

Startling in a way to see so far back—
as if we'd found between leaves of a book
a picture of ourselves from much younger days
and remembered nearly everything about it
except just why we'd put it there.

Then Saw the Problem

How do you turn into a flower of the field,
the lily clothed to make Solomon rue his glory?

What leap takes off from here towards evolution,
pointing the way to the pearly everlasting?

Eons made the flower and flowers have their agendas,
whatever the population of the field—

more than a lifetime to construct that airport.

The Kestrel

While she spoke I saw another encounter.

And then she said there was the drowning heron
who called to her from the whitewater
and another time the owl in daylight
who flew past her window more than once,
the bear who loped through her camp
when her dad died, the cloudless sky
over her mother's burial plot
where two vapor trails suddenly crisscrossed.
She would not let me go without
another word, another anecdote.
Nothing escaped her hunt for meaning, meaning.

And the kestrel swooped from the treetop,
struck the moth, and looked me in the eye.

Expected

That sense on a fall night driving home
that I will see something and must see something,
climbing the hill toward the reservoir.
I will see the shadowy buck grazing in a hollow of lawn
and his antlers emerging like a doused candelabra,
and stop the car to peer beyond the street lights
with my headlights off as he watches me and decides
to dip his face back to the dark grass.

That sense of readiness prepared
by so many unexpected things.

The man lunging onto our car in the Metro,
the doors hushing shut, the gendarmes slapping their hands
on the windows as we pulled away.
He glared at the one couple who dared to look at him
and excused himself with a barked curse.

That sense recorded in the lifted arms and curved fingers
of the Highland dancers to honor the deer's grace
as he eludes the hunter.

That sense derived from my mother
who saw an angel by her bedside as a child
and knew the ghosts who attended her
as she cleaned house were playful but indifferent.
Seeing her during her difficult recovery
naked in her diaper and helping her dress
and washing her hair, that sense that I would find
the dimple in her scalp where the prosthesis was inserted.

It gathers in the strange and makes it yours.

Spell for Encanto Creek

Tall blades of tufted grasses, keep on flowing.
Towhees like good ideas, keep on flowing.

Pooled water, black in shadow, green in sunshine,
with wild olives bending down to drink,

those figures coming daily to the bridge
to look at their two shadows on your surface,

keep them returning, keep them coming back.

Outward Bound

As when, on the interstate in the country,
you have to pull over and stop
and get out to change drivers, the hurtling forward
stops and the day opens as the car door opens,
and you are no longer moving but still, as the day moves around you,
and you see just how fast everyone else is going,
and you decide either to enjoy the field beside you, your back to the traffic,
or quickly as possible get the car going again:

So, leaving the rush of private thoughts is also
like entering an open stillness. A great halt occurs.
Someone else, talking, removes you from the inner pressure,
and either you can enjoy the release, like a field of sunflowers,
or hurry to break off
and rejoin the mental traveling that speeds you away.

The Heronry

After a year of too much face time,
I came where I could choose, instead of people,
birds and their slant gaze, water, trees and clouds,
the gossip and confidences of cat's-paw breezes
across the face of a lagoon.
I knew the place was the byproduct of money.
I knew it was peace that the state had paid for—
though only a few who knew about it prospered.
There was a bench in the sun that looked out over the shallows,
near where a black phoebe fluttered and looped
and a great egret slid one foot forward at a time in the thin water.
And there was the heronry, a thicket of slim-branched eucalyptus,
where the night herons in their black caps and sturdy patience,
like security guards, roosted and slept.
I put my eyes to binoculars, a pen on a notebook page.
Students rode by, lugging surfboards out to the point.
I heard all kinds of chatter, but always in a passing stream.

Simply to watch as other creatures lived,
stalked each other for sex, ate,
or staked their territory with frantic displays
or like cormorants dried their wings in the sun,
simply to stand apart and be something else,
the note-taking one, inconsequential,
lent me a greater peace than prayer—
to be no more than a stump or a rock,
yet too untrustworthy to nest in or light upon . . .
I'm talking about a few minutes of stillness a day
as birds did their work and, stiller than I,
the golden bush and ice plant ingested the sunlight,
the clouds, always moody, chose a single mood,
the night herons studied their dreams,
and a loneliness that I still believe was solitude
dusted me with its pollen.

13

The water twitched a little.
I pretended I had it all to myself.
I tried to observe behavior I could note in my book,
though every time I thought I'd captured a stride or wing beat,
it altered, or the hunter missed.
And I hadn't come there for knowledge, anyway.
I don't know why I came, to tell the truth,
except to be alone, though I wasn't alone and don't think I wanted
     to be.
Once the crack of a branch, falling under a bulky redtail hawk,
sent a murder of crows, like a loud black rainbow,
arcing across the lagoon. Every other bird scattered,
except the night herons, who didn't stir a bit,
hunched on single legs on single branches.
Some people in the distance pointed.
And I was glad to be there, looking where they looked.

I almost think I could write about it forever,
adding word to word like coral in a reef,
an excess of language like the genetic code, an extravagance like all
     the stars,
too much ever to be needed except
by the need for there always to be more,
that need which, when the end comes, looks past it
for woods and hills and ocean,
for fields and streets and houses and horizon,
repelled by blankness, expecting beyond sleep
the dream country and its population.

Believers, Unbelievers

Reverend "Rev" Rebenek

Waking in predawn dark with his young son,
the thought of fishing like a Christmas morning,
a flame that danced above their happy heads,
so that they had to dress an hour early
and go—go, although it was Sunday morning,
and the congregation would sit waiting, puzzled.

Then with the convicts, talking about books,
the year he had no work except volunteering,
and reading *Jonathan Livingston Seagull*
with men whose crimes he learned like the liturgy,
till all of them wanted to break out and be seagulls.

Then helping the young couple in his church
and visiting them and sharing a simple meal
the afternoon the fiercest member of the congregation
expected him to perform his daughter's wedding,
and stalked the neighborhood to find him.

And finally his wife watching him spend
on things that others needed, watching debt
sag like the overgrown gutters of their house,
until she had a need, she said, not to be married.

After a sermon in which he said the Holy Spirit
was the electricity, we were the appliances,
and proposed a ceremony of divorce
so that his marriage could end on an upbeat note,
the church turned to someone else to lead.

Failure swung past his face like leaves in fall,
the tulip poplar's leaves, the hackberry's,
and what he saw instead of the jaundiced trash

was simply change of seasons, new vocations.

Bad luck to follow preachers everyone loved,
and to have nothing yourself to give but faith,
weird sermons, poor choices of words, excitement
aimed in the wrong direction, and divorce,
abandoned in a small town in Kentucky,
again without work, again believing
all of it God's wonderful plan for your life.

Betsy Moore

The elder has called his wife from the motel,
confessing at last what she has known all along—
she who stood in the church office and told his lover
that she was trying to love her, she was trying.
The elder, a man as moral as a contract,
upright as a billboard, confident
as one of those buttons that say, "I FEEL GREAT!"
has called his wife to confess, and she is listening.
Seated at the table where she pays bills
and writes letters to her sons and looks out
through sliding glass doors at the backyard, she is listening.
Every Christmas she has poured the gifts of liquor
from his associates down the kitchen sink, every bottle.
She sings an achingly pure soprano in the church choir.
She is soon to be a grandmother. The elder,
the adulterer, will resign his position in the church,
and will not like the life he is soon to be living,
although it includes his lover, the church secretary.
Meanwhile he is confessing from the bed
where they have just made love. He is calling
his wife because his lover has told him to,
and his wife is listening. She cannot picture the look
on her husband's face, or taste his nervous sweat,
or smell the other woman on his hands,
or touch their naked bodies, and does not wish to.
But she is willing to listen, and she is listening.

Aunt Rolla

She had the softest face.
She treated it with ointment.
She'd had smallpox as a girl.
I remember how warm she was.

She treated her face with ointment.
You could see the pits and craters.
I remember how warm she was.
She would let us touch her scars.

You could see the pits and craters.
They were smooth and rosy.
She would let us touch her scars
when we were little children.

Though they were smooth and rosy,
her scars disfigured her.
When we were little children
we were afraid to touch.

Her scars' disfigurement
from smallpox as a girl
was explained, and yet she scared us
until we touched her face.

Passed On

Head of the motor pool in World War II on Saipan
Tumbled out of his jeep one night on Saipan
Head injury requiring a plate on Saipan
Story told to his wife in a letter from Saipan

Story believed when he came home from Saipan
Night of stars and a drunken ride on Saipan
Anonymous lover tumbling with him on Saipan
There was no such person with him on Saipan

Devoted father escaped from family to Saipan
Never a shred about the woman on Saipan
Plate in his head and heart put in on Saipan
Long dead old man a young man then on Saipan

Mr. Jackson

Every neighborhood has a philosopher and ours is gone. His ghost
   will walk
the pretty little mutt to the dead end and vanish in our headlights as
   we come home.

For him the departed still lived in the houses they had left.
He pointed to each one and told its annals, unsmiling but amused.

He quoted the best lines of neighbors he'd lost track of
and meditated on their whereabouts. He thought deep thoughts.

"The atom's full of emptiness," he said. "Did you know that?
And there's a message woven through the Hebrew letters of the Bible."

He kept the world on a short leash, like his mongrels, the smartest dogs,
compact and pretty as their names, though he never knew their ages.

When Pearl died he wasn't surprised. She didn't want her kibble and
   lay down.
And Taffy has outlived him—to get loose and scatter squirrels up walls
   and tree trunks.

He finished Latin but not high school, loaned me a book on Tai Chi
that had raised his energy level. I had it ready to return and meant to.

The cap, the glasses, the deep thoughts, the lump of the defibrillator
like a pack of cigarettes on his left breast—he fell out of his chair,
   watching TV.

Mr. William Jackson is dead. He found a church where he could come
   as he was.
But I have seen him Sundays in a suit and tie, escorting his pet dog
   down the street.

And I have avoided him, mornings when the talk of mystical
alphabets oppressed me, I'm ashamed to say, because I couldn't put
    two words together.

Cars have come and gone for three days. His wife has already lost
    weight
and abandoned her electric scooter, walking guests to their cars.

"He waited on her hand and foot," says a neighbor. "Now what will
    she do?"
I thought he kept the pretty little dogs as compensation.

When our street lofted the Hale–Bopp comet above us, it looked
    like a white puppy tugging at its leash.
And that spring Mr. Jackson said, "Look how that thing's made our
    dogwoods blaze."

Meg Stanley

Nightly in her dreams he rambled on.
He sat beside her in bed,

staying youthful as she aged,
and talked it out, blarney and bullshit

turning into pleading,
calling her pet names, secret things.

Every night,
the man she had three daughters with,

the man who kept failing,
and moving north,

until in Alaska's midnight sun
the whiskey seized his throat,

his car hit the child and he ran
on and out of life.

Every night for years.

And then his friend came to visit,
old college pal, preacher who married them.

And she enjoyed her first
night without dreaming of him.

And learned next morning
he'd sat beside the old friend all night in bed,

calling him
by a nickname from their youth

and urging him to sign on
to the scheme that would make them rich.

Brightlingen

At family church camp he fretted at his group meetings.
The mountain air, that light, dry, California brew,
was buoyant as froth or the rattlesnake's footless tread.
And yet in this bathing and basking atmosphere,
he put his head in his hands before his fellows
and worried, worried at how he made a living.
He made his money, fed his family, paid his mortgage,
and, still a young man, would send his children to college
because he could imagine remarkable systems,
highly efficient, intercontinental systems,
to deliver death to families like his and ours.
We children heard about him or overheard
our parents chatting at bedtime about his trouble
and other trouble. We were surrounded by trouble,
there in the sunny, shady, breezy mountains,
themselves a system of pines and underbrush
and creeks too shallow to drink from, all whispering,
all of it so good it hardly seemed possible
that among us there was one who designed systems,
miraculous systems that could demolish us.
And there were also those who feared their families,
though on vacation, feared them and wanted to flee,
and confessed as much at their group meetings, too.
We prayed in the dark. Our parents did not design systems
or admit that they feared us, not as far as we knew.
And the pines surrounded our cabin and stood at our windows
all night long and were there in the morning, too.

That Teenager Who Prowled Old Books

That teenager who prowled old books to find
any argument with a whiff of the Holy Ghost,
I meet him again in his marginalia,
which ignored the common sweat and stink and marked
those passages that confirmed what he was hunting.
There was the milk white hart of evidence, checked.
There was the hound of heaven, underlined.
And there were the hunters, in pursuit themselves,
Plato, Lucretius, Virgil, Marcus Aurelius,
who did not know he knew what they were after.
And so he missed a lot, all of it human,
even while scribbling black and blue *Eurekas!*,
bleeding through pages backwards.
It was all about something else, which he didn't see,
as philosophers mounted their lovers from behind
and felt their limbs go dead from the toes upward,
and poets kissed a mouth that fastened tight
and locked tongues and tried to catch their breath.

The Northern Lights

They were all white, passing through their stages
in sheets and ladders, rivulets and falls,
white—a dream of color or an aftermath
of color stripped to gauze and gossamer,
a white electric squall in half the sky,
epiphany for the blind, and veils of tears.
Magdalene's tears. The tears that Jesus wept.
What draws them forth? Mortality and laughter,
the sad and funny fact that you will die
and that you've made your children, they will die.
Do they hold that against you? Strangely, no.
It seems the fair result of being born
and is nobody's fault. My parents made me.
They went ahead and made me, child of love,
child of a loving union, which would end,
but which I grew up thinking would not end.
The northern lights remind me of their love.
The drama of my growing up was love
as they performed it, everyone noticing,
the scintillating cosmic imagery
of two who seemed to be made for each other,
as light is made for sheets of summer darkness,
as darkness in high summer accepts light.
Why did I ever think that they were gods?
But I didn't. I thought that they were people,
and people love each other for a lifetime.
Gods are as fickle as the northern lights.
Don't ever think of human beings you love
and need as like those shifting shimmerings,
no matter how liquescent memorable enduring
against the immortal darkness of the sky.
The northern lights will break a heart and heal it
in the same motion, raveling and unraveling.

They are the background music of creation,
the song God sang while sinking into rest,
the song descended into, words and music,
oblivious and yet ready to break hearts,
heartbreaking and yet in the end oblivious.
So I have thought about a years-ago night,
the northern lights above a northern mountain,
and how the tears came down and why, forgetting
that there is nothing oblivion won't forgive.

In a Bookstore in Hay-on-Wye

I spent the afternoon reading an old anthology,
following the subject headings. First, "God,"
poems about God, then poems about "Self,"
and, as if they followed inevitably, poems on "Nothing."
These made a kind of sense. It was the section of "It"
poems that stopped me, and then the poems about "All."

It was eccentric, to say the least, that all
the poems in this well-worn anthology
were termed "religious," and it
seemed awfully flexible. Only the poems on "God"
had a clear connection to God. Those on "Nothing"
were interchangeable with those on "Self."

In fact, the poems on "It" and "All" and "Self"
also were interchangeable. All
I could think was that there was nothing
the editor wished to share about his anthology
except what he thought about "God"
and slowly this "God" became clear as a complicated,
        uncategorizable "It."

And if that "It"
was like anything besides itself
then even the poems about "God"
could as easily have been in the section on "All"
and all of the poems in the anthology
might have more in common than they had with "Nothing."

I thumbed back through the foxed pages. Nothing
to note, except a burn mark, and even it,
on a random page of the anthology,
signified little more in itself

than wear and tear. Or was it, among all
the stains and dog-ears, a sign from God?

An accident of fire, the sort of comment God
might drop from a reader with nothing
except a smoke on his or her mind. I thought of the cinder's fall
still burning as it drifted down and alit
and left the ash-black sign of itself
on the brittle page. I reshelved the anthology.

I left the bookstore and the country, thinking about God but having
        bought nothing,
and fell to brooding back in the States about this genre of lit,
and ordered myself online a pristine but oddly unsatisfying copy of
        the anthology.

Bad Girl Singing

She took her roommate's cash,
walked out of a *supermarché*
without paying, lost her passport,
lifted another girl's and stole her boyfriend,
ditched class to see a *boules* tournament,
persuaded others to ditch with her,
so they could buy her lunch,
got sick drunk on Sundays,
arrested, threatened with deportation,
and finally, finally after her parents
were contacted in the States
and arrangements made to fly her home,
she went on our little tour
of historic sites and even there
pulled a typical stunt, distracting
everyone from the guide's good English.
Separated from our group, she stood
in the apse of the ancient church behind the altar,
singing with a voice that glowed
and brightened in the candlelit space.
She sang through her trouble and our trouble,
her lies and laziness, license and dishonesty,
our disapproval and distaste.
Unearthly at first but transmuting
the stoniness of the air, the flints
of stained-glass light, the chill,
her singing, like a lover's warmth,
entered our bodies and made us
recognize our desire was being offered back.
She sang her rejection of our rejection.
And we stood miracle-stricken, shame-blinded,
renewed by failure more than triumph.
No one excused her. She would have to leave.
But we yielded to her song.

George W. Bush

Because he felt that Jesus changed his heart
he listened to his heart and took its counsel.
When asked if he felt any of that counsel
had impacted the veterans he rode with
on a bike trek through hills and riverbeds—
some of the men without their limbs but able
to keep up despite the chafing ghost pain—
he said how honored he felt to be with them.
But no, he said, still listening to his heart,
the heart that Jesus changed, "I bear no guilt."

How much is anyone whose heart speaks for him
responsible for what his heart has told him?
The occupation of the heart is pumping
blood, but for some it is to offer counsel,
especially if it has been so changed
all that it says must finally be trusted.
Nested within the lungs, sprouting its branches,
the heart is not an organ of cognition.
But some would argue that its power is greater
than the mind's even, once the heart is changed.

And so a change of heart he believed saved him.
I hope we understand belief like that,
for there are many we would grant that mystery.
The challenge is to grant the same to him.
Perhaps we can remember one of the columnists
who often wrote as his apologist,
arguing that a convicted murderer
must still be executed for her crime,
even though she had found the Lord in prison.
Forgiveness was between her and the Lord.

If we're outraged at him or at each other,
who will come between us and our outrage?
If there's no guilt to bear, what's to forgive?
Our losses are unbearable. Our pain
will have to be the ghost of our forgiveness.

Wenlock Carston

A black man trying to teach white people,
all *Angelenos* like himself, at family camp,
how to play chess, dance *cha cha*, and understand
the savagery of their police in Watts:
He rolled his sleeves crisply above his biceps,
and guided wives beside the checkerboards
where he was taking on the thoughtful husbands
and sons and daughters who were there to learn.

After the prayer meeting one pine-cool night,
when we sang spirituals, and one good woman
who had the knack put on a descant, almost
African as at least she tried to be,
he spoke to us—I know that he felt divided,
he and his wife and children being there alone—
and when he tried to tell us what we'd done,
we whom he'd taught to dance and think, he broke down.

That compact, elegant man, in his crisp shirt,
letting us rub against him, body and mind,
who took part as I'm sure he felt was right,
among our good, inadequate white faces,
came to the point he couldn't anymore,
and standing before us, all of us happy campers,
who'd seen it all on TV and from the freeway,
he let the tears obliterate all words.

But I'm not finished yet, although he was.
Wasn't there an opportunity
to understand? It was dissolved in pity.
As Americans we want to find the solution
and move on. The evenings in those mountains
were fragrant, free from worry, soaked in hymns.

I'm speaking here of a time in the 1960s.
It won't come back. You can cry all you want.

Mickey Lucas

Our works are filthy rags in the eyes of the Lord.
And was I wrong that the waves I rode in the morning
were like our works, and so I had to give them up,
as I gave up my truancy, my long hair,
and returned to school in coat and tie with Bible?

For a time, that time, I could not watch my friends
tearing across a wave face as it Jerichoed behind them,
and not see luxury, misguided energy,
nothing like the praise from the heart that matters.
Our waves in the Lord's eyes were filthy rags.
But was that right, as I thought that it was right?

Surf fever had been a disease, but this new passion
was not a disease though it changed what I saw
in my friends, in the waves, in the mirror. In the face
of the wave I saw the living God and not a flight
from God but toward God—into a steep embrace.

Life had turned me from the single way, so I had
to leave that life—lace of salt and sand on the neck,
the teak colored tan all year, the skin of girls,
and the wild hares like eating a bag of carrots
for night vision surfing, and soul surfing
on grass that made the water sparkle and smile.

Now I surf for souls: I feel God's pleasure
when I talk to them on the strand, after they're in,
or in huddled firepit groups drinking and smoking.
I kick off my shoes and walk out on the sand,
and they will say they've heard what happened to me
and pity me—I can tell—though I offer them mercy.

Faith is like fiberglass, a rag toughened by resin.
I speak the word of God and watch the waves
break from right to left and left to right,
a script underlined with foam which I can still read—
and that I can read it still makes me stop and wonder.

The Istanbul Album

She's eating her huevos rancheros and he's showing her
his pictures from this summer. It's lovely here
in his sister's garden, and their mother can eat with her hands—
the warm tortilla and egg should be easy to chew.
Here is the Hagia Sofia. It was a church once.
And here is St. Irene's where the creed was hammered out.
Fall is really the best time in the Midwest,
spring and fall before and after hot sticky summer.
And it's September in Chicago. *Here is the Spice Bazaar.*
That's where he bought her a bag of floral tea.
Here's Taksim Square, the heart of the modern city.
And in a year—she will be gone in a year—it will explode
with raging protests over the loss of its green space.
Here's the inside of the Blue Mosque. Those tiles!
It was Ramadan. People fasted all day.
He asks her, "Don't you want to finish your breakfast?
But this is your favorite. That's why we made it for you."
Here's a picture of the crowds along the Hippodrome,
waiting to break their fast, families, couples,
groups of workers, friends, all with picnics,
like the Fourth of July. He says, "I thought you wanted
to see these. I made the album for you." *And at evening*
the muezzin would signal the hour when a white thread
could not be told from a black thread, although the lights
were on everywhere, like a fairground, and it was marvelous.
He says, "Are you finished? Do you want us to take you home?"
A cool breeze would rise from the Bosporus and swirl
among everyone like a caress, like a phenomenal blessing.
"*I* used to sew," she says. "I could thread a needle in the dark."

Another Field

Dünya Ahiretin Tarlasıdır

The world is the harvest field of the hereafter.
And the far field. And the ice field.
The debris field. And the force field.

The world is the harvest field of the hereafter.
And the waste field. And the kelp field.
And the broken field. The open field.

The world is the harvest field of the hereafter.
The playing field. And the cloud field.
The killing field. And the star field.

And the hereafter? Another field.

Friends and Wolves

The wolves are at us and our friends look on,
calling out every name in the book of wolves,
all of it, sadly, shouted in human tongues,
none of it comprehensible to wolves.

Rest on the Flight into Egypt

How can they sleep? Joseph awkwardly
pillows his head on a ledge in the sand,
and Mary between the Sphinx's stone paws
leans back with the child aglow in her lap.

Yet they are sleeping. The smoke of their fire
pays out a vanishing thread to heaven.
Their donkey grazes on bones of grasses,
his saddle a shelter for darkened sand.

There are no stars. Perhaps they have fallen,
increasing the grains of drifted sand.
But, no. It is dawn. The statue has seen it,
and so has the child—high in the east.

The donkey goes on breaking its fast.
The exhausted parents continue to sleep.
And two pairs of eyes, a child's and a monster's,
keep their watch on a world of sand.

After the painting by Luc-Olivier Merson

Walking on Water

Matthew 14

Always the same message out of Matthew.
The water Jesus walks on is life's turbulence.
He calms our trouble and lifts us up again.

To walk on water? That's what's puzzling—
     that feat of antimatter, defeat of physics,
those beautiful unshod feet of cosmic truth

     for whom the whole performance is child's play.
And unless one becomes as a little child
     the kingdom's inaccessible by any route.

That water, then, its broken surface tension,
     collision of fracturing waves, apparent chaos,
its fractals turning infinite and weaving

     the netted skin between worlds, that web
of light and gravity which underpins our faith,
     water, a substance, stormy or pacific,

we know a myriad ways to get across it.
     But simply walking on it? Literally?
How far do you think you'd go before you fell

     through that convergence between time and space?
The water Jesus walked on wasn't water
     only. It was the storm that made it rock.

Bulgarian Icon of *The Last Supper*

If they saw around his head and theirs the halos—
all would be known. And Judas without a halo
would not fool anyone. This is true of all such paintings.
But why are the two white parsnips on the table
in the foreground? The upper room crowds in
with slotted windows, spindly pillars, under a small blue dome.
Everyone's dressed in the gold of holiness, even Judas.
And in Christ's halo, the letters of his fate are legible.
Anyone looking his way had to know. But those root vegetables,
there side by side, among the three-pronged forks—
they couldn't be more accurate, less stylized.
And in those loving cups—aren't those dumplings?
Everything else is flattened into the sacred.
All lineaments are red in the clothing worn, the faces
long, lined, expressionless, are all alike.
Before each man, a scarlet triangle, like a place card,
waits, perhaps, to be plucked up and hidden.
In Bulgarian, the words for "Last Supper," somewhat ambiguous,
mean "holy or secret, enigmatic, mysterious meal."
Here, footnoted by dumplings. And a pair of parsnips.
As if to say: "Just as you eat at your house. Any night."

The Teachable Moment

John 18:38

Pilate questioned Jesus.
Jesus questioned back.
Pilate questioned him again—
the cool Socratic tack.

Their repartee was candid,
a pointed give-and-take.
It was not clear if its last word
was freely willed or fated.

When Jesus chose to answer
and give the reason why,
Pilate asked him, "What is truth?"

*

Enough about the distant posting among barbarians,
enough about having to arbitrate their quarrels,
enough about their religions—about any religion—
enough about whatever was going on at home, with the family,
when it came time for the intellectual push and pull
he had everything covered, riposte and response,
the tools of dialectic, a question for a question.
He said no more to this princeling of an obscure cause
but turned to the crowd and asked them what they wanted.
Did he win the debate? Do as fated? Make a cosmic mistake?

*

Inside me I believe there is
a Pilate questioning Jesus

and a Jesus answering.
Or no Pilate. Or no Jesus.

*

These two people, powers of their time,
faced off like a major city and an earthquake.
The city has endured so many earthquakes,
the earthquake's always virgin with a city.
One says it's coming, one must rather doubt it.
And the city shakes down on its tens of thousands.
But here's the thing, the city is rebuilt
with the same name, perhaps with earthquake codes.
The earthquake will not come again for centuries.
And the city stands again, where it has stood.
No wonder the city doubts its own destruction.
How can you live, except to doubt your death?

*

To feel your whole body is the truth,
to feel you are the truth and more than truth,
your feet, your toes, the shinbone and the knee
are true and more than true, to be the truth,
standing on your own feet, and riding hips
as true as they were ever meant to be,
the rest going upward, through the groin,
the functional, true genitals, the belly
spread with its pubic hair all true, all true,
and up the ridged divided abdomen,
between the nipples, truly loving touch,
the clavicles with their delicacy and music,
the arms and hands and fingers with their reach,
the tower of the neck, as Solomon says,
the identifiable face, *your* face,
the ears to hear both the outer and inner voices,

the mouth, the speaker of the truth, the nose,
true to its compass bearings, smelling falsehoods,
the eyes looking into the puzzled eyes
of one you've scared into urgent reasoning—
to feel that you embody the whole truth
and then to know that truth is going to be beaten,
beaten to the bone, skeletonized,
and hang like a limp rag, as dead as rope—
to be this truth completely, unadorned,
real as the hand before another's face,
and have that other still say, "What is truth?"

*

But there is more.
There's always more.
The score's not settled.
There is more.

One shuts the door.
One strikes the door,
worried, nettled,
outside the door.

What is truth for?
What is it for
for those who worry
what it is for?

Who pace the floor,
the shifting floor
of air and fury,
like a classroom floor.

Who mark the hour,
the frozen hour

of the last word,
as the first hour?

And what is power
that once was power
in an old word
with a new power?

*

The teachable moment.
The last judgment occurring
again and again as a teachable moment.
But what moment ever lasted long enough
to learn anything? This moment.

Milagro

Hammered tin the shape of the suffering part,
  the leg, the arm, the abdomen, the ear,
the hand, the mouth, the eye, the heart,
  nailed to the church wall as thanks and prayer,
the name meaning miracle and last resort.

  Touching to see them in a silvery mosaic
tacked to rough board or a seamed crosspiece
  and think that from all the parts you could construct
the human soul itself and all its griefs
  and still know that you had fallen short.

Let's put up one for drought, a speckled shield
  like a mackerel sky, and also one for famine,
a tarnished badge of ribs hung on a child,
  and one for genocide and for torture one
just like it, just like it, a blank field.

  And one is needed for the last day on earth,
a microbe milagro for the virus, and to heal
  the tsunami in its mindless setting forth
a tectonic milagro riding on molten steel,
  one the size of the earth to pin to the earth—

a miracle for the world nailed to the world.

Two Islands

Corsica

We entered under the cliffs,
at Bonifacio, just the two of us that time,
your hand on the tiller,
the hand that trembles now at your side.
They dwarfed us, as we folded sail and motored
into the slip beside the yachts,
and looked up at the town on its hilltop.
You are still upstanding, though bent a little.
The cruise ship enters the harbor,
and we reminisce with the younger couple beside us,
whose faces show a complicated response,
learning how years ago we sailed alone here
at the end of that summer, with you steering.

Santorini

On the clifftop snowy with whitewashed houses
in the one red building my wife is singing.

She is singing the Greek songs of Ravel,
her legato linking the breakage of time.

A volcano became a saint of peace
and now she lifts a note from its edge.

A lagoon turned blue in a basin of lava
and now her song floats on its light.

A caldera became a necklace of islands
and now she clasps it around her throat.

A cloud of ash turned to cloudless sky
and now the sun climbs through her voice.

In the one red building on the white-crested cliff
of a place blown apart, she is making it whole.

Boy with a Buttercup

Damn cold. Damp cold. He stands with the weans,
thick wrists jutting from blazer sleeves,
bulb-kneed, old enough to be in long pants,
cap too small, big fist holding the flower
in forefinger and thumb, under his dripping nose,
the yellow petals the only sunshine in the schoolyard
where even the red sandstone's misted with coal smoke.
And his mother, at the gate, calls to the headmistress
who watches erect at the top of the stairs,
that her Sandy's a flower for his teacher, Miss Munro.
The head cups her ear and signals for the children to file in.

Looking at that boy in memory,
wearing an outgrown uniform, or hand-me-down,
the runny nose a sign of every child in that place,
pigeon-breasted boys with weeping chilblains,
girls with eyeteeth eaten by sugar,
I have understood a century of English lit.
Raw spring of the 1950s. If he lived
he grew up to sweep the streets
or clean up children's breakfast vomit with sand
or enter the Seaforth coal mines tunneled under the firth.

And the little open-mouthed boy beside him,
the blethering, American lad, no longer exotic to classmates—
he watches as he watched everything as a child,
saying to himself that in America, this would be different.

Prosím

The scree of the chimney swifts
The façade's crawling notations
The shopper's cumbersome gifts
The mop's defenestrations

The green rust under the nails
The feuding done in secret
The dogs with docked ears and tails
The liquor served in a tea set

The graffiti on the church door
The graph of the window spider
The pickpocket's mute score
The furnace's all-nighter

The kneeling beggar's cap
The cobblestone splattered with cheese
The satchel clutched in the lap
The native word for "Please!"

Mothering Sunday

It was Mothering Sunday, so different from Mother's Day in an
    American church.
For English style the custom was both abashed and bold. They gave
    their mothers flowers—
daffodils because it was early spring—and quietly returned to quiet
    liturgy.
We watched a mother with her dirty son, a street person she seemed
    to have brought in,
although clearly he was her son, the tanned sunken profile he
    turned to us showed the family resemblance,
though the blue-black filth of his slick parka and slick hair were
    clearly all his own.
When it came time to bestow a daffodil, he shrugged and turned
    and headed for the exit.
Why had he come at all, to leave her gaping? He stalked out before
    the flowered mothers
could enjoy the drawn-out service in their honor, everyone, except
    his mother, refraining
from looking after him. So we looked at her. The flower didn't
    matter. He'd been her flower.

Tiel Burn

A minor river rises in the west,
a creek, a brook, it ambles to a sea
no greater in its way than it, a burn,
and finds its mouth where pebbles, sea coal, sticks
roll out and in and dwell as lumps in mud.
A spill of runoff from suburban farms
and neighborhoods that see it as a ditch
behind their alleyways, it passes through,
a dim phenomenon that catches light,
unseen within its cutting, a dun raveling,
where water birds trill canticles but only
to each other, if at all, and sing
of thirst and appetite and breeding there,
a minor river running through their lives—
and, I'm surprised to learn, through part of mine,
the south end of a life I left far north,
far north and east, through all these years, a quirk
of landscape which now I have seen from space
on Google Earth, yes, there, a pencil line
of pallid shadow drawing east through country
that pokes its pastoral nose into a sea
I can neither feel nor picture any more.
Where the burn empties, mudflats fly their gulls,
and, I have read, a rare duck was once seen
and noted by a birder, years ago.
Years and years ago. To get used to that
I have to keep from saying it. To feel
the time pass through as if it were my blood
I have to act as if I cannot feel it.
To understand the distance—only ten miles
in length the burn's a very minor river
descending from a spring in little hills—
I have to act as if I never knew it

was always present, always passing through,
on its way to the shifting place of change
that turns from fresh to salt, and worlds divide,
giving to the sea its gift—itself.

Polska Street

We have heard the nightingale
and guessed where it was singing,
deep in the linden trees,
a shape within a song.

At either end of nightfall
we have heard the aria
of a violated child
endowed with wings and music.

Such melody in the terrible,
and in the imaginary
so much unimaginable—
at least as we have heard it.

And yet what have we heard?
A small brown bird at twilight
calling to his mate
above the traffic noise.

Acknowledgments

My thanks to the following publications, where the poems in this book first appeared: *Able Muse, Academy of American Poets/Poem-a-Day, American Poetry Review, The Atlantic, Carolina Quarterly, Five Points, ForPoetry, Georgia Review, Great River Review, Harvard Review, The Hudson Review, Image, The Journal, Méasure, Melic Review, Miramar, The Mockingbird, The New Criterion, Plume, Rattle, Tiferet*, and *The Yale Review*.

"Bulgarian Icon of *The Last Supper*" was reprinted in *The Best Spiritual Writing 2012* (Penguin Books). "The Teachable Moment" was reprinted in *Best Spiritual Writing 2013* (Penguin Books). "George W. Bush" was reprinted in *Best American Poetry 2013* (Scribner).

I am grateful to Professor Daniel Schafer of Belmont University who gave me the translation I have used for "*Dünya Ahiretin Tarlasıdır.*"

And to Amy, always my first reader: "We have heard the nightingale . . ."

Lauren Urquhart

Mark Jarman's most recent collection of poetry is *Bone Fires: New and Selected Poems*. His honors include the Lenore Marshall Prize from the Academy of American Poets, the Poets' Prize, the Balcones Poetry Prize, and a Guggenheim Fellowship in poetry. He is Centennial Professor of English at Vanderbilt University.

Sarabande Books is a nonprofit literary press located in Louisville, KY, and Brooklyn, NY. Founded in 1994 to champion poetry, short fiction, and essay, we are committed to creating lasting editions that honor exceptional writing. For more information, please visit sarabandebooks.org.